Death is Wrong

Gennady Stolyarov II

Illustrated by Wendy Stolyarov

Gennady Stolyarov II

Second Edition

ISBN 978-0615932040

This is the book I would have wanted to have as a child, but did not. Now that you have it, you can discover in less than an hour what it took me years to learn in bits and pieces. You can instead spend those years fighting the greatest enemy of us all: death.

Gennady Stolyarov II

When I was little, numbers fascinated me. I learned to count at age 2, before I even learned to read. When I was 4 and living in the city of Minsk, I was introduced to years as a way of tracking time. I saw a shiny new ruble coin with the number "1991" written on it – one of the last coins of the Soviet Union. By then I was already comfortable with numbers up to one googol – 1 followed by 100 zeroes. But my first notion, when I learned about years, was that 1991 years were all that had been.

I recall being told that my grandfather was a child during the years "41" through "45", when the Nazis invaded the Soviet Union and he had to flee. I did not know that these numbers were abbreviations for "1941" and "1945", so I made the reasonable guess that my grandfather was around close to the beginning of time.

But I was also curious about what the passage of time would do to people. Once I asked my mother what happens when people grow up. "They go to school," she replied. "And then?"

"Then they go to university." "And then?"

"They work and get married." "And then?"

"They have children." "And then?"

"Their children have children. They retire and help raise their grandchildren." "And then?"

"Their grandchildren have children." 3 of my 8 great-grandparents were still alive at that time. "And then?"

"And then they die."

"Die? What does that mean?" "It means they stop existing. They are just not there anymore."

"But why do they die? Do they do anything bad to deserve it?" "No, it happens to everyone. People get old and then die." "It is wrong!" I exclaimed. "People should not die!"

I asked how long people live before they die. "100 years," I was told, probably to console me. I liked big, round numbers, and 100 was still somewhat big to me back then. Somehow, through that conversation, I got the notion that *everyone* lived until 100 years, and that I had a guaranteed 96 years left. I was also told that only adults can die, not children. All this was likely meant to comfort me, as the thought of dying disturbed me visibly.

Still, even 100 years did not seem enough to me. I did not know about conventional superheroes yet, though I did start reading ancient and medieval myths and folk tales. I would spend many hours making up stories of my own and jotting down quick pictures in long, thick notebooks. My superheroes were old wise men who traveled the world on magic carpets. They had exceptionally long beards, longer than my grandfather's gray beard, since they were much older. To me, a beard became a symbol of living to an old age; the older a man was, the longer a beard he got to have. I, too, decided that I would grow a beard when I could, and I would never shave it – as a reminder of a part of myself I never wanted to lose.

I specified the ages of these wise men. I remember one who was 104, one who was 115, and even one who was 140. They *all* lived past 100 years, and they flew on their magic carpets among skyscrapers that were each over 100 stories tall. They flew to the Moon and to the planets of the Solar System, which I had memorized. They defied the limits that others considered insurmountable, and they experienced adventures that, for very old men, were supposed to be impossible.

As I started to read history books and watch films, it did not take me long to find out that most people did not survive to age

100, and that, yes, even children could die. May 9, 1992, was celebrated as Victory Day – the 47th anniversary of the Soviet Union's defeat of Nazi Germany in World War II. All the television stations showed old historical films, including images of Nazi persecution of Russian civilians when the war began in 1941. I learned that the Nazis shot and hanged millions of innocent people. I found out that, in addition to dying of old age, people could be killed, and no one was invulnerable.

The old Soviet films showed that some of the "heroes" who fought back against the Nazis were younger than 15 years old. Some of these child soldiers were made to suffer horribly before they were killed, but, apparently, they did not betray their Motherland. They were praised without limit for having given their lives for their country, but to me, what happened to them was just sad. They should have tried to escape and live as long as they could, I thought. There was no glory in death, and no point in it.

The more I learned about possible ways people could die, the more alarmed I became. I realized that the risk of death was always nearby. There were so many possible illnesses – cancer, pneumonia, heart disease, diabetes – and accidents – car crashes, falls, sharp tools that slipped from one's hand – all of which could bring about death. All this made me very easy to persuade to avoid dangerous places and bad habits. Smoking and drinking alcohol were bad, because they would kill me eventually. A more immediate risk was walking on top of manhole covers, which were often only partially closed, or going by oneself to the more dangerous parts of Minsk, where crime was frequent and rising. Although I could not avoid my share of falls, scrapes, and fights with the neighborhood bullies, I got into far less trouble than most children because of my strong desire to avoid death.

One day at age five, in the late spring of 1993, I was visiting the Minsk Botanical Garden with my grandmother. We sat down on a bench overlooking a large pond where ducks and swans swam. On that sunny, temperate day, hundreds of flowers were in bloom, and I was amazed at the abundance and variety of colors in the world. "How," I asked, "could it ever be right for all this experience to just end? How could it be right that, one day, I would never again witness this beauty, or anything else, or even remember having experienced it?" After death, I understood, a person no longer is even aware of *having lived.* It is as if one never existed. I made a promise to myself then that I would wage war on death, that I would not allow my life and memories to be snuffed out.

"Whatever can be repaired gradually without destroying the original whole is, like the vestal fire, potentially eternal."

Francis Bacon (1561 – 1626), *A History of Life and Death*

During every birthday I have had since, when I was asked to make a wish, the wish was always the same: never to die, to keep living without end. This seemed to me such a clear and obvious desire that, as I grew older, I was astounded that most people did not share it. Sure, they grieved when a loved one died, and they expressed outrage when a murder was committed. Many of them took care to reduce the risks to their own lives as well. But, when talking about death *in general,* many of them seemed resigned to it eventually happening. Some would even excuse and justify death as necessary. I was bewildered that anyone would be willing to lose every sensation, every thought, every memory, every awareness of having ever existed.

When I moved to the United States at age nine, I began to notice multiple types of arguments that tried to justify human mortality.

Some said that death is not a problem, because people would continue to exist after death in heaven or some other form of afterlife. But I see no evidence that such an afterlife exists. How can a person's existence continue after the processes of the body no longer keep the mind in the brain working? I am completely certain of this life, and I would not trade certain reality for a great uncertainty.

Some said that it is better to die than to become ever older and frailer, and to live in great pain. But what if one could remain not just alive, but always young? It made sense that, if death is caused by the same problems which caused pain and frailty in old age, then the only way to get rid of death would be to undo the process of *senescence* – the decay of the body with age.

Some said that people who live forever would get bored and want to die. But, even then, I did not understand how it was possible to become bored, when there is always more to see and do. The older I became, the more possibilities I saw for spending my time.

Some said that, if people lived without end, the world would become overpopulated and run out of resources. But human population is the highest it has ever been, and most people live far longer, healthier, more prosperous lives than their ancestors did when the Earth's population was hundreds of times smaller. Technology gives us far more food, energy, and living space than our ancestors had, and the growth in population only gives us more smart people who can create even more technologies to benefit us all. Besides, humans ought to build more settlements

"The rapid progress true science now makes occasions my regretting sometimes that I was born too soon. It is impossible to imagine the height to which may be carried, in a thousand years, the power of man over matter… [A]ll diseases may by sure means be prevented or cured (not excepting even that of old age,) and our lives lengthened at pleasure, even beyond the antediluvian standard."

Benjamin Franklin (1706 – 1790), Letter to Joseph Priestley

on land, on water, underwater, and in space. Space travel could also save the human species if the Earth were hit by a massive asteroid that could wipe out complex life.

Some said that the cycle of life and death is needed for the old to make way for the new. But people are not yesterday's trash. They should not be used up and then discarded. They can think and feel, work and create. They can have both the old and the new in them, and they can continually renew their own lives.

Some said that death after senescence is natural and simply part of biology. But not all creatures senesce. Some just get older without becoming frailer. They can still suffer and die from accidents and illnesses, but if they are lucky to escape such misfortunes, there is no upper limit on their lifespans. Their chances of dying do not increase as they get older.

• Lobsters have lived for over 100 years.
• The rougheye rockfish can live for over 205 years.
• Giant tortoises are exceptionally long-lived. An Aldabra Giant Tortoise – Adwaita – lived from 1750 until March 2006. He died at age 255 after his shell cracked and he developed a wound, but he did not die of old age.
• Ocean quahog clams as old as 507 years have been observed.

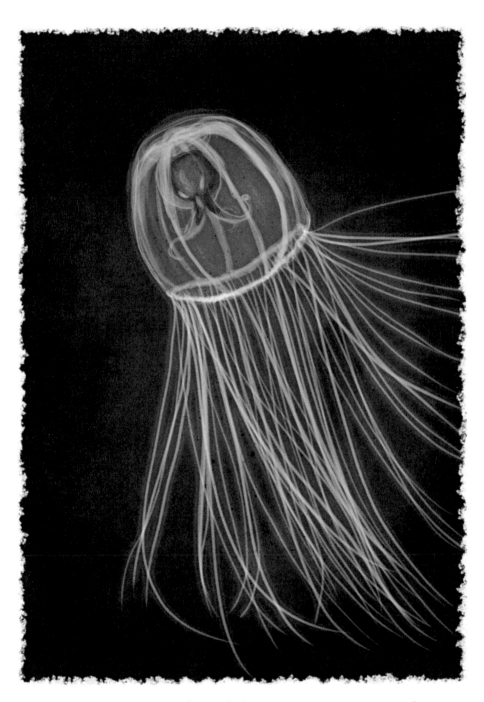

Turritopsis dohrnii, formerly known as *turritopsis nutricula*

• The Methuselah Tree, a bristlecone pine in the White Mountains of California is 4846 years old in 2013. Another ancient bristlecone pine was discovered in the White Mountains in 2012. It is 5062 years old.

The potential lifespans of these organisms could even be far greater than people have observed. They live much longer than humans, and interest in their lifespans began rather recently in our history. Perhaps they will surprise us even more. It is vital, though, to keep studying them and to help them survive for as long as possible.

One animal, a jellyfish called *turritopsis dohrnii* (formerly known as *turritopsis nutricula*), is biologically immortal. It is tiny – about 4 to 5 millimeters in diameter, barely visible to the human eye. An adult jellyfish can revert back to its infant form through a process called cell transdifferentiation. They are much simpler than we are, but we can see in them a clear example of a species that has no upper limit to its lifespan – and they do not even have science, medicine, or technology. These minuscule jellyfish have mastered the secret of eternal life! Surely, we humans can do just as well.

Unfortunately, because death has been so widespread for so

The Methuselah Tree

17

long, most people have developed excuses for it so that it does not feel so painful or scary. Arguments that one would get bored living forever, or that the world would get overpopulated, are just these kinds of excuses, which prevent people from pursuing the best possible future for them and for everyone.

What could you do if you could live for hundreds, thousands, tens of thousands of years? What could you do if you could live even longer than that?

You could read many of the greatest books ever written, and maybe even some of the not-so-great ones. And guess what? Even if you lived forever and read one entire book every day, you would *never* run out of reading materials! About 2,200,000 books are published each year, and this rate is always increasing. So no, you would never get bored if you take any interest in anything.

You could become a great composer and develop your skills to the level of Mozart or Beethoven. Someday I would like to create more compositions than Georg Philipp Telemann, who wrote the most music out of anyone who ever lived – over 3000 pieces! Telemann lived in what is today Germany, between 1681 and 1767. 86 years was long for his time, so he was able to

Galápagos Giant Tortoise

"Would it be absurd now to suppose that the improvement of the human race should be regarded as capable of unlimited progress? That a time will come when death would result only from extraordinary accidents or the more and more gradual wearing out of vitality, and that, finally, the duration of the average interval between birth and wearing out has itself no specific limit whatsoever?"
Marquis de Condorcet (1743 – 1794), *The Future Progress of the Human Mind*

set a world record in the number of compositions. To set an even bigger record, it will be necessary to live far beyond today's lifespans.

You could work in multiple professions, and retirement would not be permanent. You could earn money for 40 years, then take a break for 10 years, then try a different way of earning money – all while remaining healthy and able to enjoy life. You could become extremely rich by putting your money in the bank and letting it earn interest over a very, very long time. If you put only one dollar in the bank today and let it sit there, and the bank paid you just 1% interest each year, you would be a billionaire 2083 years from now. At 2% interest, it would only take 1047 years.

You could live to see the most amazing scientific and technological wonders, like space elevators, settlements on other planets and in orbit around them, underwater cities, and tiny nanorobots that could repair anything that gets damaged – including you. You could meet intelligent robots that could hold a conversation with you just like a human would, and you might not be able to tell the difference.

You could even live long enough to see the construction of a

Dyson sphere, a giant shell which could someday be built around an entire star to harness its energy.

You could meet your great-great-great-great-great-great-great grandchildren and tell them stories about how life was back in the day without interstellar space travel or underwater cities.

If you are adventurous, you could travel to other star systems yourself and build new settlements there. The nearest star system to our own is Alpha Centauri, which is 4.4 light-years away. This means it will take the fastest spaceships longer than 4.4 years to get there. People need to have a lot of time and patience to settle other worlds, and most would only make the journey if it did not take a huge chunk out of their lives.

You could live long enough to find out how long giant tortoises and ocean quahogs and bristlecone pines can actually live when they are observed more closely and taken care of more carefully. You would also care more than people do today about preventing waste and pollution, since you would have to personally live with the consequences hundreds and thousands of years from now.

Looking forward much farther, the solar system is not going to

"Is life not a thousand times too short for us to bore ourselves?"

Friedrich Nietzsche (1844 – 1900)

last forever on its own. In about 5.4 billion years, the Sun will turn into a huge star known as a red giant. Unless people do something about it, the Earth would become uninhabitable. Humanity needs you to help develop ways to either keep the Sun going or to spread human habitation far enough that it would not matter if some stars stopped supporting life, because people could just move somewhere else.

The possibilities for spending your time would be endless. People would no longer live life in strict stages, like going to kindergarten, going to school, working on a fixed routine, and retiring because they are too frail to work anymore. Instead, every person would have the time and abundance of choices to think about how he or she would really want to live. What are your dreams? Living without end is necessary for you to achieve them all.

But how could it be done? Humans have already succeeded in radically extending the lifespans of many small animals. Dr. Cynthia Kenyon discovered in 1993 that a mutation of one gene in the *C. elegans* worm could double the worm's lifespan. Imagine if a human could be 60 years old but look and feel like a 30-year-old person today! Since 1981, Dr. Michael Rose has been breeding fruit flies to live longer. So far he has managed to

"We must never forget that we are cosmic revolutionaries, not stooges conscripted to advance a natural order of things that kills everybody."

Alan Harrington (1918 - 1997), *The Immortalist*

extend their lifespans by four times. Imagine having the youth and energy of a 25-year-old at age 100!

Mice are promising candidates for radical life extension. As mammals, they have many similarities to us. Since their lifespans are much shorter than ours, it is possible to see the results of major life extension in a short period of time. A typical lab mouse can live for about three years. However, scientists have been able to achieve much longer lifespans. Dr. Andrzej Bartke created special genetically engineered mice that age much slower than regular mice. They can live for nearly 5 years! An achievement of this sort in humans would mean that average human lifespans could increase from about 80 years to about 133 years. Dr. Stephen Spindler took mice that were already in middle age (19 months old) and restricted their diets to achieve an average lifespan of about 3.7 years. In humans, this would be like applying life-extension therapies to a person who is 42 years old and extending that person's lifespan from 80 years to 99 years. But there are even more remarkable possibilities.

In 2004, when I was seventeen, I found out about the work of Aubrey de Grey, a man with an immensely long beard, worthy of the imagined heroes of my childhood. Dr. de Grey is a

Dr. Aubrey de Grey

biogerontologist, a scientist who studies the biology of aging. He takes a different approach from many gerontologists in that he does not see it as necessary to fully understand all the processes of aging before curing them. Rather, we need to know enough to undo the damage every decade or so, which would buy people time until the next life-extending discoveries come along.

Dr. de Grey wants to develop medical therapies to reverse biological aging in humans, so that we could just keep getting older in years while remaining biologically young. Dr. de Grey realized that there are just seven main kinds of damage involved in the aging process. These are the seven deadly things that happen to us all over time. He is working on research to combat many of these types of damage. His approach is called SENS – Strategies for Engineered Negligible Senescence. If you would like to find out more about SENS, including the details of the science involved, you can visit the website of the SENS Research Foundation, at http://sens.org, and read the Appendix of this book for a small introduction.

What I learned about the most promising scientific efforts of our time suggested to me that radical life extension could come in time to benefit me. But what could I do to help make it happen? I am not a biologist or doctor, and I did not have much money to donate. In high school and college, I tried to raise donations for the Methuselah Mouse Prize, which rewarded scientists who prolonged the lives of mice to record levels. Dr. Bartke and Dr. Spindler each received the Methuselah Mouse Prize for their work.

But because the promise of living without end was so different from what they were used to, many of my peers simply did not care, or did not think it was possible. Unlike me, many of them received large allowances and were careless with their money. They abandoned pocket change everywhere, and I diligently collected it. Over time, I was able to gather and donate $286.25, just from the coins and occasional dollar bills that these people threw away without a thought. One time, I even found a rare coin, an 1893 penny, which is worth about one dollar today. I kept it, though, to remind me that this 120-year-old penny is older than any human being currently alive. Jeanne Calment, a woman from Arles, France, currently holds the record for the longest lifespan. She lived from 1875 to 1997 for 122 years and 164 days. No other person is known to have lived past 120 years yet. This needs to change.

What can one person do? This is why I wrote this book and

why my wife Wendy helped me illustrate it. The younger you are, the better your chances are of surviving to see the breakthroughs in life extension that will one day enable people to live for 120, 150, 500, or even 1000 years. If you can live that long, then senescence will probably not be a problem for you. You would just need to be careful and avoid accidents and natural disasters. Aubrey de Grey thinks that the first person to reach age 1000 might even be as old as 70 today. But this is only a possibility. The future is never fully certain or predictable. If we want something, we need to make it happen.

If we can live to be 100 – past the upper limit I was told as a child – and then 120 – past the age of my 1893 penny – and then 123 – past the lifespan of Jeanne Calment – and then 256 – past the lifespan of Adwaita the Giant Tortoise – and then 5063 – past the lifespan of the oldest known tree – then we will know that we have achieved victory in the great war on senescence and death. If this happens, it will be because of the help that you and those like you provide in enabling humanity win this greatest struggle of all time. Death is wrong, but will you give in to the wrong, or will you fight it? Maybe the person who will conquer death… is you!

Appendix

SENS

Dr. Aubrey de Grey's approach to life extension is called Strategies for Engineered Negligible Senescence, or SENS for short. The key meaning of this term is that it would be possible to develop medical therapies to reverse biological aging in humans, so that we could just keep getting older in years while remaining biologically young. Dr. de Grey did a thorough survey of the available research on aging, and he realized that there are just seven main kinds of damage involved in the aging process. He also found out that all of these kinds of damage have been known since at least 1982, for at least 31 years. Biology has made tremendous progress since then, but scientists did not discover any new damage types. This strongly suggests that we know about the key problems that combine to create the frailty and vulnerability to disease that we associate with old age today.

So what are these seven causes of senescence – the seven deadly things? They all occur on a microscopic level, inside and outside your cells. A little bit of damage will generally not hurt you, but over the years it really adds up, which is why people become frail and die.

1. Extracellular Junk: This junk consists of misshapen proteins that gather outside cells and do damage instead of serving a useful purpose.

2. Extracellular Crosslinks: The crosslinks form when two or more previously good proteins on the outside of cells bind together like handcuffs, preventing cells from functioning properly.

3. Dysfunctional Cells: Some individual cells can become senescent, too. They fail to perform their intended function, but they are also toxic to cells around them and prevent the healthy cells from working as they should. Removing dysfunctional senescent cells can enable the healthy cells to do their jobs better.

4. Intracellular Aggregates: These are waste products within cells that gather there as a result of accidents in the course of cell metabolism, the chemical reactions that allow the cell to do its work. These waste products clog up the cell machinery and prevent it from doing its job.

5. Mitochondrial Mutations: Mitochondria are the power plants of cells, converting nutrients from food into energy. Unfortunately, this process in the mitochondria has some toxic byproducts that damage the DNA molecules in the mitochondria and hinder the mitochondria's function.

6. Nuclear Mutations: The cell's nucleus is where a person's genetic code is hosted. Over time, mutations occur to the DNA in the genetic code, leading people to be more susceptible to cancer and other diseases. Cancer is the most dangerous result, though, and discovering cures for it would go a long way toward solving this problem.

7. Cell Loss and Atrophy: Over time, the body becomes less capable of replacing cells that are damaged due to accidents and wear. Some cells kill themselves after a certain number of divisions. This can lead to weak muscles, loss of neurons in the brain, and a weaker immune system, increasing vulnerability to disease.

With healthy habits and avoidance of careless risks, your chances of living to age 75 are already quite good. But beyond that, there is still a huge element of luck involved. If you want to live much longer than this fairly common lifespan (still miserably short in my opinion), then it will be necessary to develop rejuvenation therapies, treatments which set back the body's biological clock. Imagine starting the therapy at age 40, when the major damage of senescence begins to seriously show. Your body could be returned to the condition it was in when you were 25. Then, every ten years, you would come back for another treatment. In the meantime, the treatments would improve and become more effective, cheaper, and safer. If you could survive for the first few decades after these treatments are developed, then you would have an excellent chance of surviving much longer – for 1000 years or even more. This is what indefinite life – living without any fixed upper limit – is all about.

For Further Reading

If you want to find out more about life extension and the possibilities of achieving it in our lifetimes, please visit the following websites and look around:

- SENS Research Foundation: http://www.sens.org/
- Methuselah Foundation: http://mprize.org/
- Sierra Sciences: http://www.sierrasci.com/
- Movement for Indefinite Life Extension (MILE): http://themile.info/
- Life Extension Foundation: http://www.lef.org/
- Kurzweil Accelerating Intelligence: http://www.kurzweilai.net/
- Resources on Indefinite Life Extension: http://rationalargumentator.com/RILE.html/
- Manhattan Beach Project: http://www.manhattanbeachproject.com/

Ways to Help

You can donate your computer time to participate in projects like Rosetta@home (http://boinc.bakerlab.org/),

Folding@home (http://folding.stanford.edu/), and World Community Grid (https://secure.worldcommunitygrid.org/index.jsp). A great game that helps you get personally involved in the research is Foldit: http://fold.it/. People playing Foldit have already solved long-standing puzzles that will help find cures for many diseases. I keep my computer on 24 hours each day, so that it could run many billions of calculations for research projects that predict how human proteins fold. This knowledge could be used to develop cures for illnesses ranging from cancer to Alzheimer's disease to malaria. You can do this, too. These projects are free to join, and anybody is welcome to donate computer time.

You can also talk about the importance of defeating death, write about it, and find new, creative ways to convince people to abandon the excuses that lead them to view death as an inevitable and even welcome fate, rather than as the enemy to be fought and overcome.

About Gennady Stolyarov II

Gennady Stolyarov II is, above all, an individual who seeks to use ideas to change the world. He is an actuary, philosopher, amateur mathematician, composer, poet, and futurist. He has published The Rational Argumentator (http://rationalargumentator.com/), an online magazine for world-transforming ideas, since 2002. Mr. Stolyarov's thousands of published works include articles, short stories, poems, videos, academic study guides, musical compositions, audio recordings, and fractal artworks. His online books, available for free download, include *Eden against the Colossus, Implied Consent: A Play on the Sanctity of Human Life, A Rational Cosmology, The Best Self-Help is Free,* and the *Guide to Stolyarovian Shorthand.*

Mr. Stolyarov holds the professional insurance designations of Associate of the Society of Actuaries (ASA), Associate of the Casualty Actuarial Society (ACAS), Member of the American Academy of Actuaries (MAAA), Chartered Property Casualty Underwriter (CPCU), Associate in Reinsurance (ARe), Associate in Regulation and Compliance (ARC), Associate in Personal Insurance (API), Associate in Insurance Services (AIS), Accredited Insurance Examiner (AIE), and Associate in Insurance Accounting and Finance (AIAF).

About Wendy Stolyarov

Wendy Stolyarov is, above all, a very silly person. She is also an illustrator, designer, and voice actress. She enjoys amateur cookery, cat cuddlery, and other forms of heart-warmery. While *Death is Wrong* is her first children's title, she has developed covers, layouts, and illustrations for many other books. Her art may be freely viewed by all at http://wendystolyarov.artworkfolio.com.

Made in the USA
San Bernardino, CA
09 June 2017